Brighter Grammar 3

An English Grammar with Exercises
New edition

C E Eckersley
Margaret Macaulay
Revised by D K Swan

Longman

Longman Group UK Limited,
*Longman House, Burnt Mill, Harlow,
Essex CM20 2JE, England
and Associated Companies throughout the world.*

© Longman Group UK Limited 1953, 1987

*All rights reserved; no part of this publication
may be reproduced, stored in a retrieval system,
or transmitted in any form or by any means,
electronic, mechanical, photocopying, recording,
or otherwise, without the prior written permission
of the Publishers.*

First published 1953
This edition 1987
Twelfth impression 1993

ISBN 0 – 582 – 55897 – 2

Set in 10/12 pt Linotron Times
Printed in Malaysia by CL

Illustrated by David Mostyn

Contents

(Each lesson is followed by exercises)

		page
1	Pronouns: reflexive	5
2	Pronouns: possessive, interrogative and demonstrative	9
3	Adverbs: degree, frequency and interrogative	15
4	The present perfect tense 1	21
5	The present perfect tense 2	26
6	The present perfect continuous tense	30
7	The past perfect tense	33
8	The future 1: *will*	37
9	The future 2: offering and asking	40
10	The future 3: *going to*	42
11	The future continuous tense	45
12	The future perfect tense	48
13	Commands and requests	53
14	Active and passive voice 1	57
15	Active and passive voice 2	63
16	Sentences. Clauses. Phrases	69
17	Adjective clauses 1	72
18	Adjective clauses 2: the relative pronoun	75
19	Adverb clauses	80
20	Noun clauses	83
21	Direct and indirect speech	87

Lesson One

Pronouns: reflexive

Revision (Book 1, Lessons 13–16). **Pronouns** are words that stand instead of nouns. **Personal pronouns** are used instead of nouns that mean persons or (especially *it*) animals or things. They can be singular or plural, masculine gender, feminine gender or neutral gender. A pronoun may be the **subject** or the **object**. The subjective form of many pronouns is different from their objective form. In this, pronouns are not like nouns.

Let's look in that pronoun box again and see if there are any more **pronouns**. Yes, there are three or four more kinds. Let's look at these first, the *-self*, *-selves* kind.

Lesson One

These **pronouns** always end in -*self* (or -*selves* for the plural): *myself, yourself, himself, herself, itself, oneself, ourselves, yourselves, themselves.*

The -*self* pronouns usually stand for the same person or thing as the **subject** of the sentence. Let us see some of them at work.
 I saw *myself* in the mirror.
 Be careful or you will hurt *yourself*.
 Richard helped *himself* to the cakes.
 Mary dressed *herself* carefully.
 One must be allowed to please *oneself*.
 The kitten can now feed *itself*.
 We taught *ourselves* to swim.
 The boys hurt *themselves* getting over the wall.

There is, of course, a difference in meaning between these two sentences:
 Tom hit *him*.
 Tom hit *himself*.
The action doesn't go from one person or thing to another. It comes back again – like the reflection in a mirror – to the doer of the action. These -*self* pronouns are called **reflexive pronouns**.

Emphasizing

But this is not the only work that the -*self* pronouns do. Look at these sentences.
 Jeremy washed *himself*. I know he did, I saw him, *myself*. You, *yourself*, said he looked clean and Jeremy, *himself*, said he had had a wash.
The first *himself* is quite plainly a **reflexive pronoun**; the subject *Jeremy* and the pronoun *himself* both stand for the same boy. But the others are different. They could be missed

Lesson One

out and the sentences would still make sense. They are put there to make what is said stronger, to make it more emphatic. This is the **emphatic** use of the **reflexive pronouns**.

In their emphatic use, the **reflexive pronouns** sometimes have the meaning 'alone', in which case they often have *by* with them.

I went there by *myself*.
This is an engine that goes by *itself*.
George made that model aeroplane all by *himself*.

Here are the -*self* pronouns arranged in a table.

	Singular	*Plural*
1st person	myself	ourselves
2nd person	yourself	yourselves
3rd person	himself herself itself oneself	themselves

Exercises

A Put **reflexive pronouns** into the blank spaces in these sentences.

Example: John hurt ____ when he fell.
Answer: John hurt *himself* when he fell.

1 Father cut ____ when he was shaving.
2 Mary saw ____ in the mirror.
3 We saw ____ in the mirror.
4 I taught ____ to play the piano.
5 The kitten tried to bite me, and bit ____ by mistake.
6 The poor woman threw ____ under the train.

Lesson One

7 The boys helped ____ to the cakes.
8 There are plenty of cakes here, Richard. Help ____.

B Put **reflexive pronouns** in their emphatic use into the blank spaces.

1 He did the work all by ____.
2 I saw the accident ____.
3 Mary sewed those dresses ____.
4 One can't saw a tree like that by ____.
5 You children must tidy this room ____. I am not going to help you.
6 The children tidied the room by ____.
7 Do you think, John, that you can cook the dinner by ____ today?
8 We cooked the dinner entirely by ____.
9 This machine works by ____.
10 You and Richard can do that job ____.

Lesson Two

Pronouns: possessive, interrogative and demonstrative

Possessive pronouns

Now let us have a look at the **possessive pronouns**. I want you to look back for a moment to the lessons on **adjectives** (Book 2, Lessons 4 and 5). You will remember that we had adjectives that showed possession: *my* book, *your* cat, *his* bicycle, *her* car, *our* house, *their* garden.

But in the following sentences there are some other words that show possession.

> That seat isn't *yours*; it's *mine*.
> Lend me your bicycle; *hers* is no good.
> He's wearing a hat that isn't *his*.
> That cat is *ours*.
> We spent the day with the Browns. *Theirs* was the best party I have been to.

The words *yours, mine, ours*, etc., don't qualify nouns. They show possession, and here they are standing instead of nouns; *yours* means, in that sentence, 'your seat', *hers* means 'her bicycle'. They are **possessive pronouns**.

You will quite often find the **possessive pronouns** used with *of*, like this:

> He is a friend of *mine*.

Not a friend of me as you might expect. Here are some examples:

> That dog of *yours* has been fighting again.
> There's John and that friend of *his*, going to play tennis.

9

Lesson Two

Here is a table, so that you can compare the **possessive pronouns** and the **possessive adjectives**.

Possessive adjectives	Possessive pronouns
This is *my* book.	This book is *mine*.
This is *your* book.	This book is *yours*.
This is *his* book.	This book is *his*.
This is *her* book.	This book is *hers*.
This is *our* book.	This book is *ours*.
This is *their* book.	This book is *theirs*.

Pronouns that show possession are possessive pronouns.

Interrogative pronouns

There are some pronouns that we use when we ask questions. For example,
    Who are you?
    What have you done today?
    Which of these books do you want?

Pronouns that are used to ask questions are interrogative pronouns.

Demonstrative Pronouns

Here are four pronouns whose work is to point out things.
    This is a book.   *These* are my books.
    That is a star.   *Those* are stars.

Pronouns that 'point out' are called demonstrative pronouns.

RICHARD: But you told us that *this* and *that*, *these* and *those*, *what* and *which*, were **adjectives**.
TEACHER: I did.

10

Lesson Two

RICHARD: But now you say they are **pronouns**.

TEACHER: Richard, read me the 'rule' on page 5 of Book 2.

RICHARD (reads): 'You tell what part of speech a word is by the work it is doing.'

TEACHER: Right. Now look at these sentences:

A	B
Which book do you want?	*Which* of these books do you want?
What exercises have you done today?	*What* have you done today?
This book is a good one.	*This* is a good book.
That star is called Mars.	*That* is a very bright star.
These books belong to the teacher.	*These* are the teacher's books.
Those stars are millions of miles away.	*Those* are very distant stars.

In column A, *which, what, this, that, these, those* are **adjectives** (see Book 1, Lesson 8) because they qualify **nouns**. In column B, they are pronouns because they stand instead of **nouns**. Is that clear now, Richard?

RICHARD: Yes, thank you. I understand it now.

11

Lesson Two

Exercises

A Put **possessive pronouns** in the blank spaces.

Example: We own that cat. That cat is ____.
Answer: We own that cat. That cat is *ours*.

1 I own that cat. That cat is ____.
2 You own that cat. That cat is ____.
3 He owns that cat. That cat is ____.
4 She owns that cat. That cat is ____.
5 They own that cat. That cat is ____.

B In the following sentences use the verb *be* instead of the verb *belong*. Make any other necessary changes.

Example: That house belongs to me.
Answer: That house is mine.

1 Those books belong to her.
2 That new house belongs to him.
3 These gloves belong to you.
4 That picture belongs to me.
5 That car belongs to us.
6 Those flowers belong to them.
7 Does that cat belong to you?
8 Do those toys belong to her?
9 Do these chocolates belong to us?
10 Did those chocolates belong to them?

C Put in the missing **possessive adjectives** and **possessive pronouns**.

Example: John has done ____ homework, and he's helping me with ____.
Answer: John has done *his* homework, and he's helping me with *mine*.

1 I've eaten all ____ sandwiches. Can I have one of ____?

Lesson Two

2 Tell Richard not to forget ____ book. And you mustn't forget ____.
3 George has lost ____ pen. Ask Mary if she will lend him ____.
4 We've had ____ dinner; have they had ____?
5 Richard has a dog and so have I. ____ dog and ____ had a fight.
6 Have you heard from that friend of ____ who went to Hong Kong?
7 The teacher wants you to return that book of ____ that he lent you.
8 Margaret wants to know if you've seen a pair of gloves of ____.
9 Mr and Mrs Green and a friend of ____ are coming to see us.
10 We are going to Kingston to stay with a Jamaican friend of ____.
11 Dinner has been ready a long time. I have had ____ and Mary has had ____; come and have ____ now.

D In this exercise you are going to make examples of **pronouns** and **adjectives** at work in sentences. We give you one example, and you make two more examples – different ones.

1 Make two sentences with *which* as an **interrogative pronoun**.
   Example: Here are two cakes. *Which* do you want?

2 Make two sentences with *which* as an **interrogative adjective**.
   Example: It's raining. *Which* umbrella will you take?

3 Make two sentences with *that* as a **demonstrative adjective**.
   Example: *That* bus goes to Piccadilly. Let's get on it.

4 Make two sentences with *that* as a **demonstrative pronoun**.
   Example: *That*'s our bus. Run!

Lesson Two

5 Make two sentences with *what* as an **interrogative pronoun**.
 Example: *What* do you want for supper?

6 Make two sentences with *what* as an **interrogative adjective**.
 Example: *What* time is it?

E *This* is a story about a well-known American millionaire, John D. Rockefeller. A friend of *his* told the story. *This* friend said that though Rockefeller gave away millions to help other people, *he* never liked to spend money on *himself*.

One day *he* went to stay at a hotel in New York and asked for the cheapest room *they* had.

'*What* is the price of the room?' he asked. The manager told *him*.

'And *which* floor is it on?' Again the manager told *him*.

'Is *that* the lowest priced room you have? I am staying here by *myself* and only need a small room.'

The manager said, '*That* room is the smallest and cheapest *we* have,' and added, 'But why do you choose a poor room like *that*? When *your* son stays here, *he* always has *our* most expensive room; *yours* is *our* cheapest.'

'Yes,' said Rockefeller, 'but *his* father is a wealthy man; *mine* isn't.'

Note the words in italics. Say which are **adjectives** and which are **pronouns**, and give the kind in each case. Here is the first one as an example:

Example: *This* – pronoun, demonstrative

Lesson Three

Adverbs: degree, frequency and interrogative

Revision. **Adverbs** are used with **verbs** to tell *how* an action is done (**adverbs of manner**), or *when* an action is done (**adverbs of time**) or *where* an action happens (**adverbs of place**). They are often made by adding *-ly* to the **adjective**; but there are some exceptions. **Adverbs** generally follow the **verb**. Phrases that do the work of adverbs are called **adverb phrases**.

Adverbs of degree

You have learned that **adverbs** are used with, or 'modify', **verbs**. But there is one kind of adverb that modifies **adjectives** and other **adverbs**. Look at these sentences.

Tom did a *very* difficult exercise.

That hat is *too* big for you.

Yes, it is *rather* large.

Dinner is *almost* ready.

She has a *really* beautiful face.

All these words are answers to such questions as 'How difficult?' 'How big?' etc., and you will notice that they are used with the adjectives *difficult*, *big*, etc., to tell the degree of 'difficulty', 'bigness', etc. They are **adverbs of degree**.

Some **adverbs of degree** can modify **adverbs**.

Richard ran *very* quickly.

Lesson Three

He arrived *too* soon.

He answered the question *quite* easily.

Some **adverbs of degree** modify **verbs**.

I *hardly* know him.

That *nearly* hit me.

I *quite* understand.

We have *nearly* finished this exercise.

Adverbs of degree modify verbs, adjectives and other adverbs.

Adverbs of frequency

There are other adverbs that tell us 'how often'. They are called **adverbs of frequency**. Here are some examples:

I *never* see him now.

I have *never* seen him.

We *sometimes* meet him on the bus.

They *usually* go home at weekends.

He doesn't *often* go to the cinema.

Lesson Three

You can *always* find her in her office.

Notice the position of these adverbs in the sentence. Write them before most verbs, but after the 'peculiars'.

Other **adverbs of frequency** are written at the end of the sentence.
    I went there only *once* or *twice*.
    He comes here *daily*.
    The meetings are held *weekly*.

Interrogative adverbs

Some adverbs are used to ask questions. They are **interrogative adverbs**.
    Where are you going?
    Why did you do that?
    When will he come here?

Comparison of adverbs

You will remember that **adjectives** have degrees of comparison (Book 2, Lessons 6 and 7). You have the same thing with adverbs, but only with **adverbs of manner**.

Positive	Comparative	Superlative
fast	faster	fastest
early	earlier	earliest
well	better	best
badly	worse	worst
quickly	more quickly	most quickly
happily	more happily	most happily

17

Lesson Three

Adverbs and prepositions

Sometimes the same word may be used as an **adverb** or as a **preposition**; it depends on the work the word is doing. If it governs a **noun** or a **pronoun**, it is a **preposition**.

   A mouse ran *past* (preposition) her.

   It ran *past* (preposition) the door.

   Mary was frightened when a mouse ran *past* (adverb).

Here are some more examples:
   The car ran *over* (preposition) a snake.
   A plane flew *over* (adverb), and we watched it.

   He went into the room *before* (preposition) me.
   I have been to this place *before* (adverb).

   We heard the burglar *inside* (preposition) the room.
   It's raining. Come *inside* (adverb).

   The bucket went *down* (preposition) the well.
   Sit *down* (adverb).

Exercises

A Use one of the **adverbs of degree** in the box for each space in the following sentences and then say whether the **adverb** that you choose modifies a **verb**, an **adjective** or another **adverb**. We have done the first one for you.

---

very too rather almost quite nearly more most less
terribly entirely completely just hardly slightly

18

Lesson Three

Adverb	Modifies
1 very	**adjective** difficult

1 This exercise is not ___ difficult.
2 John speaks French ___ well.
3 The explorers ___ died of thirst.
4 He drove the car ___ fast in that busy street.
5 I have ___ finished my work.
6 I think she answered that question ___ cleverly.
7 Be careful. You ___ killed me.
8 I am ___ sorry to hear that your father is ill.
9 This is one of the ___ difficult questions to answer.
10 What he said was not ___ true.
11 I have ___ forgotten what he said.
12 Your work is ___ important than your games.
13 I know him ___.
14 I ___ know him at all.
15 Richard ought to listen ___ and talk ___.

B The words in *italics* in the following sentences are all **adverbs**. Say what kind each one is.

Example: John *sometimes* writes to me.
Answer: sometimes – adverb of frequency

1 Richard ran down the field *quickly*.
2 We went to see a friend *yesterday*.
3 Wayne plays football *well*.
4 I *quite* agree, he plays *very well*.
5 We had tea and played games *afterwards*.
6 *Where* are you going *today*?
7 I have *often* made that mistake.
8 *Why* don't you work *more carefully*?
9 I used to see him *once* or *twice* a week; *now* I *never* see him.
10 *When* will he learn not to drive his car *so* fast?

Lesson Three

C Say whether the words in *italics* are **adverbs** or **prepositions** and give reasons for your reply.

Example: The gate was open, and the cars went *through*.
Answer: through – adverb, modifies *went*

1 The music got louder as the band drew *near*.
2 I stood *near* Richard in the crowd.
3 Your name will be called *before* mine.
4 You ought to have told me that *before*.
5 *Inside* that box there are valuable jewels.
6 I will never go *inside* that house again.
7 It's very nice to be *outside* when the sun is shining.
8 He stood *outside* the door, and listened to what was going on *inside*.
9 The horse ran *round* the race course.
10 The big wheel turned *round* slowly.
11 If you can't climb *over* the wire fence, get *under* it.
12 You can go *under*; I'm going to climb *over*.

Lesson Four

The present perfect tense 1

Revision. **Verbs** are words that express an action or a state of being. There is always a **verb** in the **predicate** of a sentence and this verb agrees with its **subject** in number and person. Verbs that take an **object** are **transitive verbs**; verbs that don't take an object are **intransitive verbs**.

The form of a verb shows:
1 the time (present, past or future) when an action happens, happened, or will happen, and
2 the completeness or incompleteness of an action. The **present continuous tense** is used for an action that is still going on. The **simple present tense** is used for a repeated or habitual action. The **past continuous tense** is used for an action that was continuing in the past.

Verbs form their **negative** in two ways:
1 By adding *not* with the **base** form (the method of the 'peculiars').
2 By using *do* (*does*, *did*) with *not* and the **base** form (the method of all verbs except the 'peculiars').

Verbs that form their **simple past tense** and **past participle** by adding *-d*, *-ed*, or *-t* to the **base** form are **regular verbs**. Verbs that form their past tense and past participle by changing their vowel are **irregular verbs**.

TEACHER: Come here, John. I want you to help me with this lesson. I am going to ask you to do some simple things and then I'll ask you a few questions. First, will you open the door, please? (*John does so.*) Now what have you just done, John?

Lesson Four

JOHN: I have opened the door.

TEACHER: Good. I'll write your answers on the blackboard.

> I have opened the door.

(*To Harry*) What has John just done, Harry?

HARRY: He has opened the door.

TEACHER: Now write your name on the blackboard. (*He writes 'John'.*) What have you just done?

JOHN: I have written my name.

TEACHER: What has John done, Richard?

RICHARD: He has written his name.

TEACHER: And what have I just asked you, Richard?

RICHARD: You have asked me a question.

TEACHER: John, shake hands with Richard. What have John and Richard just done, Mark?

MARK: They have shaken hands.

TEACHER: Now, all the class, close your books. What have you all just done?

CLASS: We have closed our books.

TEACHER: Now, look at these sentences on the board. John, put a line under all the verbs. (*John does so.*)

I <u>have opened</u> the door.
I <u>have written</u> my name.
He <u>has opened</u> the door.
He <u>has written</u> his name.
We <u>have closed</u> our books.
You <u>have asked</u> me a question.
They <u>have shaken</u> hands.

Notice that all these verbs have two parts. The first is *have*

Lesson Four

(or *has*); the second is the **past participle**.

The form of a verb shows two things (Book 2, Lesson 12): 1 when an action happens; 2 whether the action is finished or not. In the sentences that we have just written down, it is quite clear that the action is finished. But the speaker's interest is in the result of the action:

I have opened the door. (Look. It's open.)
I have written my name. (Look. There it is on the board.)
You have asked me a question. (And now I'm answering it.)

So the present perfect tense is used when we are thinking more about the present result than about the past action.

In the examples above, we know the time of the action from the context. In other cases, the **present perfect tense** is often used with **adverbs** or **adverb phrases** that tell us about the time.

Here are some examples. Notice the position of the **adverbs** and **adverb phrases** in the sentences.

just	Richard has *just* answered the question.
already	I have *already* opened the door.
(not) yet	Have you seen the Tower of London *yet*?
	I haven't finished lunch *yet*.
up to now	I have done English grammar for two years *up to now*.
since . . .	I haven't eaten anything *since* early this morning.
for . . .	We haven't had a letter from them *for* a year.
nearly	We have *nearly* finished supper.

The present perfect tense is formed by using *have/has* and a past participle.

Lesson Four

Exercises

A Write down the **past participles** of these verbs. Add (R) for a **regular verb** or (I) for an **irregular verb**.

Example: ask
Answer: asked (R)

1 write	6 ride	11 think	16 break
2 catch	7 know	12 sell	17 choose
3 freeze	8 eat	13 give	18 wake
4 open	9 see	14 throw	19 bring
5 drive	10 get	15 teach	20 pay

B One verb for each of these sentences is in brackets in its **base** form. In some cases there is an **adverb** or **adverb phrase** as well. Write the sentences down with the **verb** in the **present perfect tense**.

24

Lesson Four

Example: Look. John ___ his name on this page. (already – write)
Answer: Look. John *has already written* his name on this page.

1 I ___ a picture. Do you like it? (just – draw)
2 The cat ___ its milk. (not yet – drink)
3 The train from Paris ___. (already – arrive)
4 She ___ her letter. (nearly – finish)
5 I ___ all the cakes (already – eat)
6 Those cars ___ an accident. (just – have)
7 You ___ a mistake. This is the wrong word. (make)
8 John ___ his bicycle to his brother Tom. Tom is very happy. (give)
9 We ___ him ___. (not since Monday – see)
10 My friends ___ the Pyramids. (never – see)

25

Lesson Five

The present perfect tense 2

The **present perfect tense** forms its **negative** by putting *not* after *have* (or *has*). It forms its **interrogative** by changing the order of the **subject** and the verb *have*. (You would expect this of course, because *have* is one of the 'peculiars'.) Here are some examples:

You *have opened* the door. (affirmative)
You *haven't opened* the door. (negative)
Have you *opened* the door? (interrogative)

Mary *has been* to the zoo. (affirmative)
Mary *hasn't been* to the zoo. (negative)
Has Mary *been* to the zoo? (interrogative)

I *have taught* you this before. (affirmative)
I *haven't taught* you this before. (negative)
Have I *taught* you this before? (interrogative)

26

Lesson Five

Comparison of the present perfect and simple past tenses

Let's compare the **present perfect tense** and the **simple past tense**. You remember the actions we spoke about *yesterday*?

John opened the door *yesterday*.

After that, he wrote his name.

Then I asked a question.

John and Richard shook hands *a few minutes after that*.

Then you all closed your books.

That was yesterday. The **adverbs** and **adverb phrases** *yesterday, after that, then, a few minutes after that* show that the sentences are about the past. We use the **simple past tense** of the verbs. We sometimes use an adverb or adverb phrase, but sometimes the **context** and the **simple past tense** tell the hearer or reader that our interest is in the past.

The following **adverbs** and **adverb phrases** of time are often used with the **simple past tense**.

an hour ago	last month	yesterday
ten minutes ago	last year	on Tuesday
two months ago	last week	in 1982
ten years ago	last summer	then

The following **adverbs** and **adverb phrases** of time are often used with the **present perfect tense**.

just	since yesterday
yet	since last week
already	since 1982
up to now	

27

Lesson Five

The present perfect tense is used when we are thinking more of the present result ('up to now') than about the past action.

The simple past tense is used when we are thinking of an action completed in the past.

Exercises

A Make the following sentences (a) **negative**, and (b) **interrogative**. Some are in the **present perfect tense** and some are in the **simple past tense**.

Example 1: He has opened the door.
Answer: (a) He hasn't opened the door.
        (b) Has he opened the door?

Example 2: He opened the window.
Answer: (a) He didn't open the window.
        (b) Did he open the window?

1 I have finished the work.
2 He has written a letter.
3 Joyce has drunk her milk.
4 They have understood the lesson.
5 Richard has gone to the zoo.
6 I finished the work yesterday.
7 He wrote a letter last week.
8 Lloyd drank his orange juice this morning.
9 They understood the lesson on Monday.
10 Richard went to the zoo last week.

B Supply either the **present perfect tense** or the **simple past tense**. Put the adverbs in the correct position in the sentence. (See Lesson 3.)

1 I just (tell) you the answer.
2 I (tell) you the answer yesterday.

Lesson Five

3 George never (fly) to Japan up to the present.
4 John and Richard just (go) away.
5 She already (answer) the letter.
6 She (answer) it on Tuesday.
7 John and David (go) away five minutes ago.
8 I (read) that book in the summer holidays.
9 The baker (sell) now all his cakes.
10 He (sell) the last one half an hour ago.

Lesson Six

The present perfect continuous tense

You remember the **present continuous tense** and the **past continuous tense**:
   I *am learning* English grammar now (present continuous).
   I *was learning* English grammar a year ago (past continuous).

Well, you can also have a **present perfect continuous tense**:
   I *have been learning* English grammar for two years.
It means 'up to now' and so is present perfect continuous. Here are some more examples. As you see this tense is made by using the *-ing* form of the **verb** (learn*ing*) with *have* (*has*) *been*.

Lesson Six

Mr Thomas *has been teaching* in this school for twenty years.

Have you seen Richard? We*'ve been looking* for him all the afternoon.

I*'ve been working* on this model engine for six weeks. It's nearly finished now.

It*'s been raining* for two days. Do you think it will ever stop?

George is a hard worker. He*'s been digging* in the garden all morning.

The soldiers are tired; they*'ve been marching* since early morning.

'Is Mary at home now?' – 'No, she*'s been staying* with her aunt in London for the last two months.'

You*'ve been studying* the present perfect continuous. I hope you understand it now.

In these examples, the contracted form *it's* = it has; *he's* = he has; *she's* = she has. (Don't get this *'s* mixed up with *'s* = *is*.)

The present perfect continuous tense is used to express an action that began in the past and is still continuing.

Exercises

A Change the following sentences from **present continuous** to **present perfect continuous**. Add phrases from the box to show the time.

---

all day, all the afternoon, since breakfast time, since last June, for two years

---

1 I am learning English grammar.
2 The teacher is teaching in this school.
3 We are looking for Richard.
4 Fred is working on his radio set.
5 It is raining hard.

Lesson Six

6 We are gathering apples.
7 They are living in Kingston.
8 The cat is sleeping in front of the fire.
9 The birds are singing in the woods.
10 Father is writing letters.

B Fill in the blank columns. The first one is done for you.

Present continuous	Past continuous	Present perfect continuous
1 I am speaking.	I was speaking.	I have been speaking.
2 He is working.		
3 She is sewing.		
4 It is snowing.		
5 You are learning.		
6 We are studying.		
7 They are digging.		
8 The soldiers are fighting.		
9 The house is burning.		
10 The sun is shining.		

Lesson Seven

The past perfect tense

Look at these two sentences:
   Ali learned English. He came to England.
Both these actions happened in the past, so we use the **simple past tense**, *learned* and *came*.

But suppose we want to show that one of these actions happened before the other one. Suppose we want to say that before he came to England, Ali learned English. Then we use the **past perfect tense** for the action that happened first, and we use the **simple past tense** for the other action. We say:
   Ali *had learned* English before he came to England.

The **past perfect tense** is formed like the **present perfect tense**, but instead of using the **present** form *have* (*has*), we use the **past** form, *had*.

Lesson Seven

For another example, we are going to a football match, but we are late. When we arrive at the football field, the teams are already playing. Then when we tell somebody about it afterwards, we say:

When we reached the field, the game *had started*.

One action (the game starting) happened before the other action (our arrival on the football field). The earlier action is in the **past perfect tense** (*had started*); the later action (*reached*) is in the **simple past tense**.

Here are some further examples.

Before the fire-engines arrived, the fire *had destroyed* the house.
When Margaret *had finished* her homework, she turned on the radio.
I *had* already *got* home before it began to rain.
Richard got a new exercise book yesterday because he *had filled* his old one.
The children came to the party at 4 o'clock yesterday; but before that, Mary and Eric Lee *had decorated* the room, Mrs Lee *had baked* cakes, and Mr Lee *had bought* a small present for everybody.

The past perfect tense is used to show that one action happened before another action in the past.

Exercises

A Join the following pairs of sentences so that the **verb** in one part is in the **past perfect tense**. Add *when* or *before*.

Example: (a) John arrived at the party. (b) Fred left.
Answer: When John arrived at the party, Fred had left.

1 (a) John studied French. (b) He went to Paris.
2 (a) We arrived at the cinema. (b) The film started.

Lesson Seven

3 (a) Richard ate all the cakes. (b) Mark arrived home.
4 (a) The army commander studied all the maps of the district. (b) He made the attack.
5 (a) The gardener finished digging the garden. (b) He put in some cabbage plants.

B Here is a story. Rewrite it putting all the verbs in brackets into the **past perfect tense**. Ask yourself why it is in the past perfect.

One good turn deserves another

One evening Green was driving along a lonely country road. He (draw) £100 from his bank in London, and he (put) it in his pocket before he began his journey.

At the loneliest part of the road, a man in badly-fitting clothes stopped him.

'Can I come with you to the next town?' the man asked.
'Yes,' Green said. 'Get in.' And he drove on.

As he talked to the man, Green learned that he (be) in prison for robbery and (break out) of prison two days before. Green was very worried at the thought of the £100 that he (put) in his pocket. Suddenly he saw a police car and had an idea. He just (reach) a small town where the speed limit was 30 miles an hour. He pressed down the accelerator and drove the car as fast as it would go. He looked back and saw that the police car (see) him and (begin) to chase him. After a mile or so the police car overtook him and ordered him to stop. A policeman got out and came to Green's car.

Green (hope) that he could tell the policeman about the escaped robber, but the man took a gun out of his pocket and put it to Green's back. The policeman took out his notebook and pencil and said he wanted Green's name and address.

Lesson Seven

'Can't I come with you to the police station?' Green asked. But the policeman said, 'No, I want your name and address now. You will have to appear at the police station later.'

So Green gave the policeman his name and address. The policeman wrote it down, put his notebook and pencil back in his pocket and gave Green a talk about dangerous driving.

Green started up his car again and drove on. He (give up) all hope of his £100 but suddenly the passenger said he wanted to get out. Green stopped the car; the man got out and said, 'Thanks for the ride. You've been good to me. I'd like to give you this in return.' And he handed Green the policeman's notebook.

While the policeman was talking to Green, the thief (steal) the notebook.

Lesson Eight

The future 1: *will*

In an earlier lesson (Book 2, Lesson 10) you saw how we use *will* and the **base** form of the **verb** for the **future tense.**

| I will
You will
He will
We will
They will | be twelve years old next year. |

Some people use *shall* for the 1st person: *I shall be, we shall be*.

The **negative** is formed by adding *not* (*will* is one of the 'peculiars'). *Will not* is often shortened to *won't*.

| I *will not* (*won't*)
You *will not* (*won't*)
He *will not* (*won't*)
We *will not* (*won't*)
They *will not* (*won't*) | be twelve until next year. |

The negative *shall not* is often shortened to *shan't*:
    I *shan't* be twelve until next year.

Lesson Eight

The **interrogative** is formed by **inversion**. (Book 2, Lesson 18)

| Will you
Will he
Will they | be twelve years old next year? |

Here are some more examples of the use of the **future tense**.
I hope *it won't rain*; if it does, *we'll have to* stay in.
You won't need an umbrella.
Will you come with us on our walk?
No, *I'll stay* at home and get the tea ready.
Even if it rains *you won't get* very wet.
You're wrong there. I think that if it rains *we'll get* wet through.

Lesson Eight

The future tense is used for actions expected to happen in the future.

Exercises

A Write these sentences with *will* or *'ll* in the blank spaces.

1 I ___ be fourteen years old next week.
2 We ___ be late if we don't hurry.
3 He ___ be thirteen years old on Tuesday.
4 You ___ be late if you don't hurry.
5 ___ he open the door for us?
6 ___ you come to our house for tea?
7 John ___ come if you ask him.
8 ___ you ask him to come?
9 I think we ___ have rain this afternoon.
10 ___ your friends come and have a game?

B Change the following into the **future tense**. Change words like *today* and *yesterday* into *tomorrow* or *next week*, where necessary.

1 Mr Green drives the car to London.
2 Mr Lee gives a science lecture.
3 The students learn science from him.
4 I went to London yesterday.
5 John went to London yesterday.
6 I am fifteen years old today.
7 Wayne is eleven years old today.
8 We saw our friends last week.
9 They stayed with us last Christmas.
10 It rained yesterday and I got wet. (Begin 'I expect . . . ')

39

Lesson Nine

The future 2: offering and asking

In the **interrogative** table on page 38 we left out *I* and *we*, the 1st person.

If a question is an **offer**, we use *shall* for the 1st person:
  Shall I open the window?
  Shall we come with you?
  Shall I make you a cup of coffee?

If we ask a question to try to find out what somebody else wants, we may use *shall* for the 1st person plural:
  What *shall we* do this evening?

Sometimes this *shall* is used in a **suggestion**:
  What do you want to do this evening? *Shall we* go to the cinema?
  Shall we listen to the radio?

In all other cases, we use *will* for the 1st person future, just as we do with the 2nd and 3rd persons:
  Will I get a letter from you?

Lesson Nine

> *Will we* see you at the theatre?
> *Will I* pass the examination?
> *Will we* get wet if it rains?

(There is more about *if* sentences in Book 4, Lessons 3 and 13–14.)

Exercises

A How do you make these offers?

Example: to carry Mary's bag
Answer: Shall I carry your bag, Mary?

1 to shut the door
2 to pour out tea for your mother
3 to telephone for a taxi for Mr Shah
4 to drive Mrs Jones to the station
5 to lend your pencil to Tom

B How do you make these suggestions?

Example: Suggest to Mary that you go to the concert together.
Answer: Shall we go to the concert, Mary?

1 Suggest to John that you share a taxi.
2 Try to persuade your friend to swim across the river with you.
3 Suggest to Susan that you and she try the new teashop.
4 You want to play tennis this evening. Suggest a game to Richard.
5 Suggest to Jack that you and he stop walking and have a rest.

Lesson Ten

The future 3: *going to*

We can express future action in another way, and that is by using *going to*. Look at these examples.
   Richard says he *is going to* work hard next year.
   I *am going to* write a letter to my uncle today.
   Mr Green *is going to* sell his car.
   We *are going to* finish our homework after supper.

Look carefully at those examples. You will see that in every case *going to* expresses *intention*.
   Richard intends to work hard: 'I'*m going to* work hard,' he says.
   I intend to write to my uncle: 'I'*m going to* write to him.'
   Mr Green plans to sell his car: he'*s going to* sell it.
   We have made up our minds to finish our homework: 'We *are going to* finish it.'
If there is an intention about the future, we can use *going to*.

We can also use *going to* if there is a **cause** in the present:
   It'*s going to* rain. (I can see the black clouds.)
   RICHARD: It'*s going to* be a very good party. (Richard has seen the cakes that his mother has made.)
   TOM: I'*m going to* have a bad cold. (Tom already has the first signs of a bad cold. Tom doesn't intend to have a cold. He just knows that it is coming.)
In such cases it is also probable that the action will happen soon.

The *going to* future usually expresses intention or present cause.

Lesson Ten

Exercises

A Rewrite the following sentences using *(be) going to* instead of *will*. There is one sentence that can't be changed. Can you find which one it is?

1 My father will buy me a bicycle for my birthday.
2 Our house will be painted next week.
3 They will leave Trinidad tomorrow.
4 We will grow apples in our garden.
5 If I see him again, I'll recognize him.
6 How will you open the box?
7 Won't you have one of these cakes?
8 Won't Mary sing a song for us?
9 Will Mark and Richard play with us tomorrow?
10 Won't George and William play with us tomorrow?

Lesson Ten

B Rewrite the following sentences for future action, (a) using *will* (or *'ll*); (b) using *going to*. Replace the present or past time expressions by a future time expression.

Example: He did the work yesterday.
Answer: (a) He *will* do the work tomorrow.
   (b) He*'s going to* do the work tomorrow.

1 I wrote to him last week.
2 His uncle gave him a bicycle for his birthday last month.
3 They sold their house last year.
4 Richard worked hard last term.
5 Did Richard work hard last term?
6 What time did you have dinner?
7 Margaret sang a song at the last concert.
8 They built a new school in 1982.
9 Didn't you go to see him yesterday?
10 Didn't Richard play football on Tuesday?

Lesson Eleven

The future continuous tense

A conversation between John, Richard, Lloyd and Michael

JOHN: My father is taking me with him to Paris.
RICHARD: Oh, you are lucky! I wish I could go to Paris. When are you going?
JOHN: Next week. This time next Friday *I'll be getting* into the car to go to the station.

LLOYD: And *we'll be walking* to school!
RICHARD: And *the teacher will be waiting* for us with another lesson on English grammar!
MICHAEL: Yes, while we are learning grammar, *John will be speeding* on his way to Paris. Lucky John!
LLOYD: While we are doing our homework, what *will you be doing*, John?
JOHN: I expect *I'll be having* dinner on the train.
RICHARD: I've never had dinner on the train. What time do you get into Paris?
JOHN: If the train is on time *we'll be drawing* into the

45

Lesson Eleven

platform just about the time you are getting up in the morning.

MICHAEL: I hope *you won't be feeling* too tired after being up all night.

JOHN: *I'll be feeling* too excited to feel tired.

LLOYD, RICHARD, MICHAEL: Well *we'll be thinking* about you next Friday evening.

JOHN: Thanks. And *I'll be thinking* about you.

In that conversation you have had eleven examples of the **future continuous tense**.

The verbs are formed by using the simple future (*I will, you will*, etc.) with *be* and the *-ing* form of the verb. Here are all the forms of the **future continuous** of *walk*:

Affirmative	Interrogative	Negative
I will be walking.	Will I be walking?	I won't be walking.
You will be walking	Will you be walking?	You won't be walking.
He will be walking.	Will he be walking?	He won't be walking.
We will be walking.	Will we be walking?	We won't be walking.
They will be walking.	Will they be walking?	They won't be walking.

The future continuous tense expresses an action still continuing in the future.

Exercises

A Write out the **future continuous tense** (affirmative, interrogative, and negative) of the verb *write*.

Lesson Eleven

B Change the **subjects** of the following sentences from 1st person (*I, we*) to the 3rd person subjects given in brackets.

1 I'll be thinking about you. (John)
2 We'll be having dinner on the train. (John and his father)
3 I'll be walking to school. (Henry)
4 We won't be getting into the car. (The others)
5 I won't be feeling excited. (The others)

C Answer the questions, using the conversation in this lesson.

Example: What will John be doing next Friday?
Answer: He'll be getting into the car to go to the station.

1 What will John's friends be doing next Friday?
2 What will the teacher be doing?
3 What will John be doing while his friends are learning grammar?
4 What will he be doing while they are doing their homework?
5 What will John's friends be doing when he is arriving in Paris?

47

Lesson Twelve

The future perfect tense

A conversation between Mrs Campbell, Margaret and Jan

MRS CAMPBELL: Margaret, I want you to go to the baker's before six o'clock. I have to do some work, but *I'll have done* it in about an hour, and I need a loaf of bread for supper.

MARGARET: Can I go after six o'clock, Mother? I want to see the history programme on TV and *it won't have finished* by six o'clock.

MRS CAMPBELL: I'm sorry, but *the baker's shop will have closed* by the time the TV programme finishes.

JAN: I'll go, Mother. I don't want to see the TV programme, and *I'll have written* my homework before six o'clock.

MARGARET: Oh, thank you, Jan. *I won't* even *have begun* my homework at six o'clock, but I'll begin it as soon as supper is over.

MRS CAMPBELL: I hope you will. *We'll have had* supper and *we'll have cleared* the table by half-past seven, so you can do an hour's work before bed-time. *Will you have done* it all by half-past eight?

MARGARET: Oh, yes, *I'll have finished* everything by eight o'clock. Thank you again, Jan.

Now here we have another (and the last) of the ways of expressing future action, the **future perfect tense**. You can see nine examples of it in that conversation.

The **future perfect tense** tells us something that will have happened at or before a certain time in the future.
   At six o'clock the baker *will have shut* up his shop.
   Before bed-time Margaret *will have completed* her homework.

Lesson Twelve

This tense is made by using *will* (*I will, you will*, etc.), together with *have* and the **past participle**.

Here are all the forms of the **future perfect** of the verb *write*.

Future perfect

Affirmative	Interrogative	Negative
I will have written.	Will I have written?	I won't have written.
You will have written.	Will you have written?	You won't have written.
He will have written.	Will he have written?	He won't have written.
We will have written.	Will we have written?	We won't have written.
They will have written.	Will they have written?	They won't have written.

Lesson Twelve

The future perfect tense expresses an action that will have been completed at or before a time in the future.

In a context of future time, the **future perfect tense** expresses action in the past. Look at this group of sentences about tomorrow afternoon.

> We'll meet at the Jacksons' at about five o'clock tomorrow afternoon. By that time, we*'ll have had* tea. We won't want anything to eat or drink before eight. So we'll go for a good long walk. By eight we*'ll have worked up* an appetite. We'll be able to enjoy a big supper.

At 5 o'clock tomorrow 'tea' will be in the **past**. At 8 o'clock the walk, working up 'an appetite', will be in the **past**.

Here is a table of the ways of showing time that you have met. We will use the verb *walk*.

	Simple	*Continuous*
1 Present	a I walk	b I am walking
2 Past	a I walked	b I was walking
3 Future	a I will walk	b I will be walking

	Perfect	*Perfect continuous*
1 Present	c I have walked	d I have been walking
2 Past	c I had walked	d I had been walking
3 Future	c I will have walked	d I will have been walking

Here are examples of all those tenses. The numbers and letters are those in the table you have just looked at.

1 a *I walk* five kilometres every day. It takes one hour.
   b *I am walking* now, and I'll end my walk at 4 o'clock.
   c It's 4 o'clock, and *I have walked* five kilometres.
   d It's 3.30, and *I have been walking* since 3 o'clock.

2 *a I walked* five kilometres yesterday. I started at 3 o'clock.
  b I was walking when you saw me at 3.30.
  c At 4 o'clock *I had walked* five kilometres, and I stopped.
  d At 3.30 yesterday *I had been walking* for half an hour.

3 *a I'll walk* five kilometres as usual tomorrow. I'll start at 3 o'clock.
  b I'll still *be walking* at 3.30.
  c I'll have walked my usual five kilometres by 4 o'clock tomorrow.
  d By 3.30 tomorrow *I'll have been walking* for half an hour.

Exercises

A Try to make a table of **tenses** like the one on page 50, using the verb *write*.

B Suppose you are an author. You write one thousand words every day. You start at 8 o'clock and you stop at 12 noon. Can you make examples like the examples of the tenses on page 50 and above? Your first example might be:

1 *a* I write 1000 words every day. It takes four hours.

C Rewrite the following sentences putting the verbs that are in brackets into the **future perfect tense**.

1 By half-past seven we (have) supper.
2 The baker's shop (close) by tea time.
3 By the end of the year I (read) three of Shakespeare's plays.
4 Before his next visit he (be) to Jamaica.
5 I (finish) this work before you go away.
6 By this time next week you (take) your examination.
7 We (leave) the house before you get back.

Lesson Twelve

8 When you get back from Egypt, I expect you (see) the Pyramids.
9 The game (start) before we reach the field.
10 I hope it (stop) raining before we have to go.
11 When we see you again we (buy) the new car.
12 He (finish) the building of the house before summer.
13 The birds (fly) away before winter comes.
14 At Christmas, Mr Chung (teach) here for fifteen years.
15 I hope you (not forget) all about the future perfect by the next lesson.

Lesson Thirteen

Commands and requests

Look at these **commands** or orders.
>In the name of the law *open* the door.
>*Come* here and *speak* to me.
>*Don't make* a noise.
>*Run*!

Sometimes the **verb** in a **command** is said to be in the **imperative**.

With a **request** we often add *please*.
>Please *don't forget* to write to me.
>*Don't make* a noise, please.
>Please *give* your sister my best wishes.

53

Lesson Thirteen

The **verb** in a **command** always has the same form as the **base** (Book 2, Lesson 20).

Base	Command
take	Take.
speak	Speak.
go	Go!
do	Do.

You will notice that the **command** form of the verb usually hasn't any subject. We sometimes say that the subject of the command is *you* 'understood'.

In **commands** there is generally no subject (that's why their heads are missing!).

REQUEST: PLEASE DON'T SHOOT

COMMAND: PUT YOUR HANDS UP

(You met **commands** in Book 1, Lesson 10, and you also looked at **statements** there.)

	Subject	Verb	Object
Statement	I	open	the door.
Command	–	Open	the door.

A **statement** can be changed to a **question**, or it can be given **negative** form.

I bought a stamp.
Did you buy a stamp?
You didn't buy a stamp.

A **command** can have a **negative** form, with *Don't* (sometimes *Do not*), but it has no **interrogative** (question) form.

Lesson Thirteen

We can also make more polite requests using the 'peculiars' *can, could* and *would*.

> *Can you* give me a lift?
> *Could you* help me with this exercise?
> *Would you* shut the door, please?

Exercises

A Write down the following sentences and put after each whether it is a **statement**, a **question**, a **command** or a **request**. Put a question mark (?) where necessary in your answer. The first sentence is done for you.

1 I will close the door. (statement)
2 Close the door.
3 Don't make a noise.
4 I promise not to make a noise.
5 Please be as quiet as you can.
6 Be here at five o'clock without fail.
7 I will be here at five o'clock.
8 Will you be here at five o'clock.
9 Write your name here, please.

Lesson Thirteen

10 What is your name.
11 I want you to write your name here.
12 Write your name here at once.
13 Take these books away.
14 Have you taken those books away.
15 Don't take those books away.
16 I haven't taken the books away.
17 Write these sentences out carefully.

B Use **commands** to tell somebody how to (a) make a fire; (b) get to the school or the station or the post office; (c) clean his or her shoes.

C Write **commands** in the **negative** form telling someone not to:

1 do their (his or her) work carelessly.
2 come to the class with dirty hands.
3 copy from Carl's book.
4 leave the door open.
5 kick the dog.
6 eat chocolate in the class.
7 forget their books tomorrow.
8 write their exercise in pencil.
9 be silly.
10 frighten the baby.

Lesson Fourteen

Active and passive voice 1

Revision. **Subjects, predicates, objects** (Book 1, Lessons 11 and 12).

The word or group of words that we speak about in a sentence is called the **subject**. The subject is the 'doer' of the action.

The **predicate** of a sentence is the word or group of words that tells us something about the **subject**.

The **object** of a **verb** is a **noun** (or **pronoun**) that tells us the person or thing that the action of the verb happened to. The object is the 'receiver' of the action.

Verbs that have an object are called **transitive verbs**. Verbs that don't take objects are called **intransitive verbs**.

You may remember that in Book 1 (Lesson 12) you had this sentence:
   The dog killed a rat.
And you were told that *the dog* was the **subject** of the sentence, and *a rat* was the **object**. The dog did something; it was the 'doer' of the action. The rat had something done to it; it was the 'receiver' of the action.

Very often (as in that sentence) the **subject** is the 'doer' of the action. But not always. Sometimes we put the sentence the other way round, and the **subject** is the 'receiver' of the action. For example I could say:
   A rat (subject) was killed by the dog.
The *rat* didn't do anything; it was the 'receiver' of the action.

57

Lesson Fourteen

When the subject of the sentence is the 'doer' of the action, we say the verb is in the active voice.

When the subject of the sentence is the 'receiver' of the action, we say the verb is in the passive voice.

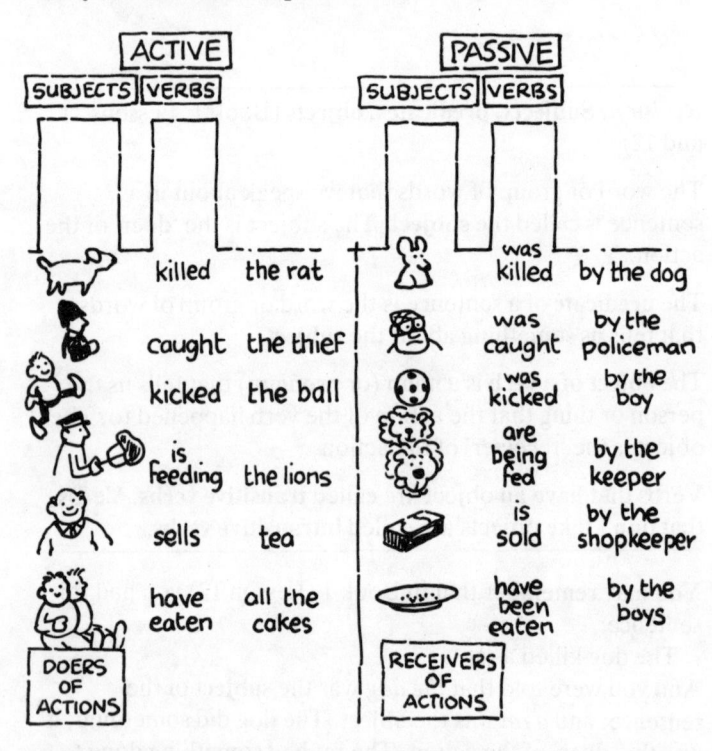

ACTIVE		PASSIVE	
SUBJECTS	VERBS	SUBJECTS	VERBS
(dog)	killed the rat	(rat)	was killed by the dog
(policeman)	caught the thief	(thief)	was caught by the policeman
(boy)	kicked the ball	(ball)	was kicked by the boy
(keeper)	is feeding the lions	(lions)	are being fed by the keeper
(shopkeeper)	sells tea	(tea)	is sold by the shopkeeper
(boys)	have eaten all the cakes	(plate)	have been eaten by the boys
DOERS OF ACTIONS		RECEIVERS OF ACTIONS	

Here are some more examples.

Active voice
Lynette sang a song.
The policeman caught the thief.
The teacher taught the class.

Passive voice
A song was sung by Lynette.
The thief was caught by the policeman.
The class was taught by the teacher.

Lesson Fourteen

The boys kicked the ball.	The ball was kicked by the boys.
Did you write this letter?	Was this letter written by you?
Did you answer the question, Richard?	Was the question answered by you, Richard?
Somebody else did that.	That was done by somebody else.

In all those examples, the **subject** in the **passive** sentence is **singular**, so we used the **singular** verb *was* and the **past participle** (*sung, caught, written,* etc.) of the verb.

Here are some examples where the **subject** of the **passive** sentence is **plural**, so we use the **plural** verb *were* and the **past participle** (*eaten, answered, built*).

Active voice	*Passive voice*
The boys ate all the cakes.	All the cakes were eaten by the boys.
Grace answered all the questions.	All the questions were answered by Grace.
The same man built both those houses.	Both those houses were built by the same man.

Only transitive verbs can be used in the passive voice.

Can you see why this is? Well, look again at these sentences.

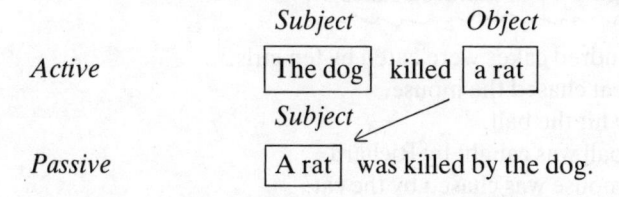

Active Subject [The dog] killed Object [a rat]

Passive Subject [A rat] was killed by the dog.

The **subject** in the **passive** sentence is formed by the **object** in the **active** one. But if the verb isn't a **transitive** one there won't be any **object**!

59

Lesson Fourteen

Exercises

A Say which is the 'doer' and which is the 'receiver' of the action in the following sentences. We have done the first one for you.

'Doers'	'Receivers'
1 ten girls	A hundred cakes

1 A hundred cakes were eaten by ten girls.
2 The cat chased the mouse.
3 Mary hit the ball.
4 The ball was caught by Richard.
5 The mouse was chased by the cat.
6 The train was pulled by a powerful engine.
7 A powerful engine pulled the train.
8 The wind blew two big trees down.
9 Two big trees were blown down by the wind.

Lesson Fourteen

B Draw four columns like this. Sentences 1 and 2 are done for you to show you the method. Answer the others in the same way.

No.	Subject	Doer or Receiver?	Voice of verb
1	The bird	Doer	Active
2	A nest	Receiver	Passive

1 The bird built a nest.
2 A nest was built by the bird.
3 The boys did the exercises.
4 The exercises were done by the boys.
5 The shoes were made by the shoemaker.
6 The shoemaker made the shoes.
7 Velma caught the ball.
8 The ball was caught by Velma.
9 The poem was learned by Margaret.
10 Many people heard the noise of the explosion.
11 The match was won by our team.
12 Margaret learned the poem.
13 The noise of the explosion was heard by many people.
14 Mary knitted these gloves.

C Change the following sentences from **active voice** to **passive voice**.

Example: Mary wrote that letter.
Answer: That letter was written by Mary.

1 I took the book.
2 Richard threw a stone.
3 Richard broke the window.
4 The horses pulled the big wagon.
5 The thief stole a ring.
6 Mark cooked the dinner.
7 The postman delivered the letters.
8 Did you write these letters?

Lesson Fourteen

9 Did you cook the dinner, Mark?
10 Did you break the window, Richard?

D Change the following sentences from **passive voice** to **active voice**.

1 The car was repaired by the mechanic.
2 The book was taken by George.
3 The dinner was cooked by Mrs Green.
4 The desk was broken by William.
5 The shots were fired by the soldiers.
6 These letters were written by my secretary.
7 Was this cabbage grown by you?
8 Was this ring stolen by the thief?
9 Were the shots fired by the soldiers?
10 Were these letters written by my secretary?

Lesson Fifteen

Active and passive voice 2

In the last lesson, all the examples of the **passive voice** were in the **past tense**.
   A nest *was built* by the bird.
But you can have the **passive voice** with any of the tenses that you have already learned.

The **passive voice**, as you have seen, is made by using a part of the verb *be* and the **past participle**; and the different forms of the **passive** are made by using different parts of the verb *be*. Here are some examples of various tenses.

63

Lesson Fifteen

Active	*Passive*

Simple present tense

The grocer *sells* tea.	Tea *is sold* by the grocer.
An electric fire *warms* the room.	The room *is warmed* by an electric fire.
Frost *kills* these flowers.	These flowers *are killed* by frost.
Cats *eat* mice.	Mice *are eaten* by cats.
Do cats *eat* mice?	*Are* mice *eaten* by cats?

Future tense

We *will finish* the work.	The work *will be finished* by us.
The teacher *will help* us.	We *will be helped* by the teacher.
The teacher *will correct* our work.	Our work *will be corrected* by the teacher.
I'm afraid the fire *will destroy* those houses.	I'm afraid those houses *will be destroyed* by the fire.
Will the cat *catch* the mouse?	*Will* the mouse *be caught* by the cat?

Present perfect tense

| The boys *have eaten* some of the cakes. | Some of the cakes *have been eaten* by the boys. |
| *Have* the boys *eaten* some of the cakes? | *Have* some of the cakes *been eaten* by the boys? |

Past perfect tense

| The boys *had eaten* some of the cakes before the party began. | Some of the cakes *had been eaten* by the boys before the party began. |
| *Had* the boys *eaten* some of the cakes? | *Had* some of the cakes *been eaten* by the boys? |

Future perfect tense

| The grocer *will have closed* his shop by six o'clock. | The shop *will have been closed* by the grocer by six o'clock. |

Lesson Fifteen

Present continuous tense
The farmer *is ploughing* the field.

The field *is being ploughed* by the farmer.

Past continuous tense
The farmer *was ploughing* the field.

The field *was being ploughed* by the farmer.

Future continuous tense
All next week the workmen *will be painting* our house.

All next week our house *will be being painted* by the workmen.

Leaving out the 'doer' of the action

Quite often when you are using the **passive voice** it is not necessary to put in the 'doer' of the action. In fact it would sound rather unnatural if you did. The following sentences will illustrate this. We would usually leave out the parts given in brackets [   ].

Active	*Passive*
People speak English all over the world.	English is spoken all over the world [by people].
Do people speak English all over the world?	Is English spoken all over the world [by people]?
Somebody built this house in 1500.	This house was built in 1500 [by somebody].
You must answer all the questions on the paper.	All the questions on the paper must be answered [by you].
Must I answer all the questions?	Must all the questions be answered [by me]?
They blamed me for something I hadn't done.	I was blamed [by them] for something I hadn't done.
Someone printed this book in Hong Kong.	This book was printed in Hong Kong [by someone].

Lesson Fifteen

Did someone print this book in Hong Kong?   Was this book printed in Hong Kong [by someone]?

Here is a summary of all the forms for the passive voice, illustrated by the verb *show*:

	Active	Passive
Simple present	he shows	he is shown
Present continuous	he is showing	he is being shown
Present perfect	he has shown	he has been shown
Simple past	he showed	he was shown
Past continuous	he was showing	he was being shown
Past perfect	he had shown	he had been shown
Future	he will show	he will be shown
Future continuous	he will be showing	he will be being shown
Future perfect	he will have shown	he will have been shown

Exercises

A Change these sentences from **active voice** to **passive voice**. Keep the same **tense** in each case. Leave something out of your answers to numbers 11, 12, 13, 14, 16, 18, 29.

(a) Present tense
 1 The girl rings the bell.
 2 Everybody forgets that.
 3 The teacher corrects our exercises.
 4 Mrs King controls a big business.
 5 The wind blows the clouds away.
 6 Does the wind blow the clouds away?
 7 Does the girl ring the bell?

66

Lesson Fifteen

(b) Present continuous
8 Mary is cooking the dinner.
9 Mr Eckersley is teaching that class.
10 The soldiers are defending the city.
11 They are examining the new student now.
12 They are sending Mr Shah abroad on business.
13 They are moving troops to the battle area.

(c) Present perfect
14 Somebody has broken the window.
15 The cat has caught a mouse.
16 Somebody has left on the electric light all night.
17 Most people have heard this story.
18 Has somebody broken the window?
19 Have the pupils finished the exercises?

(d) Past continuous
20 Our soldiers were driving back the enemy.
21 The wind was blowing the clouds away.

(e) Past perfect
22 The shot had frightened the birds.
23 Lightning had struck the house.

(f) Future tense
24 The postman will deliver the letters.
25 Will the postman deliver the letters?
26 I will finish the work.
27 We will spend the money.
28 Shall we spend the money?
29 People will forget it after a few weeks.

B Change these sentences from **passive voice** to **active voice**. Keep the same **tense** in each case. You will have to supply a **subject** for your answers to numbers 6,7,8.

1 The letters are delivered by the postman.
2 That is forgotten by everybody.

Lesson Fifteen

3 The clouds are blown away by the wind.
4 That was forgotten by everybody.
5 The city is being defended by the soldiers.
6 Mr Brown is being sent abroad on business.
7 A battleship is being sent to the war area.
8 Is the new student being examined now?
9 This chair has been broken by someone.
10 Everything that was needed has been done by George.

Lesson Sixteen

Sentences. Clauses. Phrases

Revision (Book 1, Lesson 10). A group of words that makes complete sense is a **sentence**. A sentence may make a **statement**, ask a **question**, give a **command** or make a **request**. A **sentence** has a **finite verb** in it (Book 2, Lesson 20); a **phrase** hasn't. Sentences may be joined together by **conjunctions** (Book 1, Lesson 19).

As you know, a **sentence** must have a **verb** in it. A sentence that has only one verb in it is called a **simple sentence**. These are simple sentences:

The boy opened the door. (statement)
Did the boy open the door? (question)
Open the door, please. (request)
Open that door at once. (command)

A sentence that is made of two or more **simple sentences** joined by a **conjunction**, or **conjunctions**, is called a **compound sentence**. These are compound sentences:

| The boy opened the door | and | walked into the room. |

| John works hard | but | Richard is lazy. |

| Shall I write to him | or | will you telephone? |

| John went to the baker's shop for a loaf | and

| Ellen helped her mother in the house, | but

| Margaret sat listening to the radio. |

Each of the sentences in a **compound sentence** makes

69

Lesson Sixteen

complete sense by itself, but we don't always repeat the **subject** if it is the same as the subject of the first sentence. For example, *the boy* or *he* is left out of the second part in this sentence:

The boy opened the door and walked into the room.

The sentences in a **compound sentence** are all of the same importance. The joined sentences of a **compound sentence** are sometimes called **co-ordinated clauses**. The co-ordinated clauses of a compound sentence could stand by themselves (sometimes with the subject supplied).

The boy opened the door. He walked into the room.

But there are some clauses that are not able to stand by themselves. They contain a verb (as all clauses do) but they make complete sense only when they are used with another clause – a **main clause** – to form a **complex sentence**. These clauses are called **dependent clauses**. We will consider them more fully in the next few lessons. Meanwhile remember that:

A dependent clause is a sentence that does not make complete sense by itself. It depends on another clause – a main clause – for its full meaning. Another name for dependent clauses is **subordinate clauses**.

Exercises

A What is (a) a **simple sentence**; (b) a **compound sentence**; (c) a **dependent clause**?

B Make each of the following pairs of **simple sentences** into a **compound sentence**. Leave out a word or two where necessary.

1 The boy closed the door. He walked away.
2 Richard works badly. He plays games well.

Lesson Sixteen

3 The children finished their lessons. They went home.
4 I like learning grammar. I don't like doing the exercises.
5 We come to school on Friday. We have a holiday on Saturday.

Lesson Seventeen

Adjective clauses 1

An **adjective**, as you know (Book 1, Lesson 6), limits the meaning of a **noun**.

I like a *good* story.
That is a *clever* boy.
Is this your *lost* kitten?
We helped the *shipwrecked* sailors.

But instead of these **adjectives**, we could use a **clause** that does the same work – that limits the meaning of the **noun**. For example:

I like a story | that is good | .

That is a boy | who is clever | .

Is this your kitten | which was lost | ?

We helped the sailors | who were shipwrecked | .

Each of these **clauses** (*that is good; who is clever; which was lost; who were shipwrecked*) does the work of an adjective. But none of them makes complete sense by itself. These **clauses** make complete sense only when they are with the other clause – the **main clause**. So they are **dependent clauses**. And, because they do the work of an adjective, they are called **adjective clauses**. The other clauses on which they depend for their meaning (*I like a story; That is a boy; Is this your kitten?; We helped the sailors*) are called **main clauses**.

You can have other kinds of **dependent clauses** as well as adjective ones. We shall meet these later.

Lesson Seventeen

A main clause and one or more dependent clauses together make a complex sentence.

Here are some examples of **complex sentences**. The **dependent adjective clauses** are all in boxes, with arrows to indicate the noun they refer to.

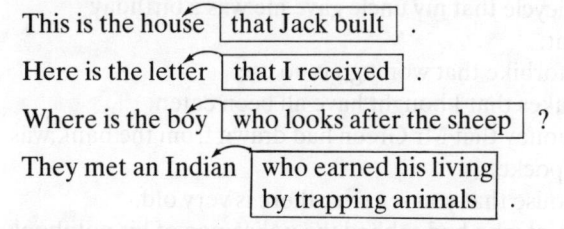

This is the house ⌐that Jack built⌐.

Here is the letter ⌐that I received⌐.

Where is the boy ⌐who looks after the sheep⌐?

They met an Indian ⌐who earned his living by trapping animals⌐.

Sometimes the **dependent adjective clause** divides the **main clause**.

The house ⌐that Jack built⌐ has fallen down.

The letter ⌐that I received⌐ is in my pocket.

The boy ⌐who looks after the sheep⌐ is fast asleep.

The adjective clause goes as near as possible to the noun it qualifies.

The **adjective clause** *that Jack built* qualifies *house*; so put it next to *house*.

The **adjective clause** *that I received* qualifies *letter*; so put it next to *letter*.

The **adjective clause** *who looks after the sheep* qualifies *boy*; so put it next to *boy*.

Lesson Seventeen

Exercises

A What is (a) a **complex sentence**, (b) an **adjective clause**, (c) a **main clause**?

B Write out these sentences and draw a box round the **dependent adjective clause**. Put an arrow to show the word that it qualifies. We have done the first one for you.

1. This is the bicycle ⌐that my uncle gave me⌐.
2. Do you know anyone who wants to buy a motorbike?
3. Here are the cakes that I bought.
4. Mr Green was returning home with the money that he had put in his pocket.
5. The bicycle that my uncle gave me was a birthday present.
6. A motorbike that won't go is no use.
7. The cakes that I bought have all been eaten.
8. The money that Mr Green had drawn from the bank was in his pocket.
9. The house that you see over there is very old.
10. The thief who had robbed the policeman of his notebook gave it to Mr Green.

Lesson Eighteen

Adjective clauses 2: the relative pronoun

You know now what **adjective clauses** are. Let us see how they are formed.

Here are two **simple sentences**:
That is the lady. She drives the school bus.

You can make those two **simple sentences** into one **compound sentence** by joining them with the **conjunction** *and*, like this:
That is the lady *and* she drives the school bus.

But here is another way to join them:
That is the lady who drives the school bus.

Now we have made the two **simple sentences** into a **complex** one. *That is the lady* is the **main clause**; *who drives the school bus* is a **dependent adjective clause**.

The relative pronoun

Notice how we made that **complex sentence**. If you compare it with the **compound** one, you will see that instead of *and* (a conjunction) and *she* (a pronoun) we have used one word, *who*, that does the work of *and* and *she*. The word *who* is a **pronoun**, because it stands instead of *she*; it is also a **conjunction** because it joins together (or 'relates') the two clauses. It is called a **relative pronoun**.

75

Lesson Eighteen

A relative pronoun does the work of a pronoun and a conjunction.

It stands instead of a **noun** and also joins an **adjective clause** to another clause in a **complex sentence**.

The two most commonly used **relative pronouns** are *who* (used for people) and *that* (used for people and things). You will also meet *which*, used for things, but nowadays it is not so common as *that*. Here are examples to show you how these **relative pronouns** join **simple sentences** together to make **complex** ones. Remember to put the **adjective clause** next to the noun it qualifies.

That is the lady. That lady drives the school bus. (simple sentences)

That is the lady *who/that* drives the school bus . (complex sentence)

Here are the passengers. They want to travel by this plane. (simple sentences)

Here are the passengers *who/that* want to travel by this plane . (complex sentence)

I have a book. It teaches English grammar. (simple sentences)

Lesson Eighteen

I have a book | *that* teaches English grammar | . (complex sentence)

The book teaches me grammar. It is a new one. (simple sentences)

The book | *that* teaches me grammar | is a new one. (complex sentence)

The lady drives the school bus. She is called Mrs Jones. (simple sentences)

The lady | *who/that* drives the school bus | is called Mrs Jones. (complex sentence)

TEACHER: Now I will give you two sentences and I want you to write them down and join them by using a **relative pronoun**. One of the sentences will then be a **main clause**, the other a **dependent adjective clause**. Here are the sentences:

    The lady drives the school bus.
    She has a special licence for it.

TEACHER: Now, Richard, read what you have written.

RICHARD (*reads*): The lady drives the school bus that has a special licence for it.

TEACHER: So the bus has a licence? What have you written, Neville?

NEVILLE: The lady who drives the school bus has a special licence for it.

TEACHER: That, of course, is the right answer. Which is the adjective clause, Richard?

RICHARD: *who drives the school bus*

TEACHER: Right. And what noun does that qualify?

RICHARD: *lady*

TEACHER: Yes. Then put it next to *lady* and not next to *bus*. Tell me the rule again, Richard.

RICHARD: The **adjective clause** goes as near as possible to the **noun** it qualifies.

Lesson Eighteen

Leaving out the relative pronoun

You will meet a lot of **adjective clauses** without a **relative pronoun**. For example, instead of
> Tell us about the people that you saw and the food that you ate.

you will hear or read:
> Tell us about the people you saw and the food you ate.

In Book 4, Lesson 1 we will show you how to leave out **relative pronouns** to make **adjective clauses** of this kind.

Exercises

A Answer these questions.

1 What are the two most commonly used **relative pronouns**?
2 What work is done by a **relative pronoun**?
3 Which **relative pronoun** can be used for persons and things?

B Make each of these pairs of **simple sentences** into one **complex sentence** by using a **relative** pronoun.

Example: Fred Brown has a dog. It is called Jock.
Answer: Fred Brown has a dog that is called Jock.

1 This is the girl. She is going to sing a song.
2 Do you like the bicycle? My uncle gave it to me.
3 I have lost the pen. I bought it yesterday.
4 Richard lives in a house. It has a big garden.
5 I have finished the exercises. The teacher told us to do them.
6 These are some apples. They grew on my tree.
7 I saw the man. He won the prize.

Lesson Eighteen

8 They heard about the battle from a soldier. He had been wounded.
9 We had a friend. He was a famous writer.
10 The girl is going to sing a song. She is called Grace.
11 The bicycle was for my birthday. My uncle sent it.
12 The pen wrote very well. I bought the pen yesterday.
13 The exercises are in this book. The teacher told me to do them.
14 The apples grew on my tree. You are eating them.

Lesson Nineteen

Adverb clauses

Revision. **Adverbs** are words that we use with **verbs**. **Adverbs of manner** tell *how* an action was done; **adverbs of time** tell *when* an action was done; **adverbs of place** tell *where* an action happened (Book 1, Lesson 17).

Adverb clauses of manner

I want you to examine these **complex sentences**. Each sentence has a **main clause** and a **dependent clause**. So that you can recognize it more easily, the **dependent clause** is printed in *italics*.

John did that work *as it should be done*.
The man ran *as if wolves were chasing him*.
Answer the questions *as you have been taught*.
He fought *as a brave man should fight*.

It is quite clear that these clauses are not like the ones in Lesson 17. They do not qualify a **noun**: they limit the meaning of the verbs *did*, *ran*, *answer*, and *fought*. That is, they are doing the work of **adverbs**. They are **adverb clauses**. They answer the questions: '*How* did John do the work?' '*How* did the man run?' '*How* must you answer the questions?' '*How* did he fight?'.

They are doing the work of **adverbs of manner**, so they are **adverb clauses of manner**.

Lesson Nineteen

Adverb clauses of time

Here are some more **adverb clauses**.
   The thief ran away *when he saw the policeman*.
   When I have finished my work, I'll go out to play.
   The tooth stopped aching *when the dentist came in*.
   A cold wind sprang up *just as the sun was setting*.
   She decided to wait *until the train arrived*.

In these sentences the **dependent clause** tells us *when* the thief ran away, *when* the speaker will go out to play, *when* the tooth stopped aching, *when* the cold wind sprang up, and up to *what time* she decided to wait.

They are **adverb clauses of time**.

Adverb clauses of place

Let us now examine another group of sentences.
   Mary put the meat *where the cat couldn't reach it*.
   The sailors went *where they expected to find the treasure*.
   Where there are flowers, you will generally find bees.
   Wherever Fred goes, Jock is sure to go.

These clauses answer the questions: '*Where* did Mary put the meat?' '*Where* did the sailors go?' '*In what place* will you generally find bees?' '*Where* is Jock sure to go?'.

These clauses are **adverb clauses of place**.

An adverb clause is one that does the work of an adverb.

Clauses that tell 'how' an action is done are **adverb clauses of manner**; those that tell 'when' an action is done are **adverb clauses of time**; those that tell 'where' an action happens are **adverb clauses of place**.

81

Lesson Nineteen

Complex sentences containing **adverb clauses** can be analysed like this:

Main clause	Adverb clause	Kind of adverb clause	Work done by adverb clause
John did that work	as it should be done.	Manner	modifying the verb 'did'
I'll go out to play	when I have finished my work.	Time	modifying the verb 'will go'
Mary put the meat	where the cat couldn't reach it.	Place	modifying the verb 'put'

Exercises

A What work does an **adverb clause** do? What kinds of **adverb clauses** do you know? Say what each kind does.

B Analyse the following **complex sentences** in the style shown on this page.

1 When we arrived at the football field, the game had started.
2 Richard left dirty footmarks wherever he went.
3 Kick the ball hard as Richard did.
4 Don't handle those cups and saucers as if they were made of iron.
5 I'm standing where I can see the game.
6 You can't come in here while we are having a lesson.
7 As soon as the boys came into the room, the noise began.
8 Use a paint-brush as I showed you yesterday.
9 Everywhere I looked, there were dirty footmarks.
10 Our friends had arrived when we got home.

Lesson Twenty

Noun clauses

Now we come to the last kind of **dependent clause**, the **noun clause**. You can guess by now that a **noun clause** will be one doing the work of a **noun**. A noun is very often the **object** of a verb (see Book 1, Lesson 12). Here are some sentences where the **object** is a noun:

	Object
Fred dreamed	a dream.
I know	arithmetic.
Mary said	a few words.

Now instead of using nouns for the objects of those verbs we'll use a **clause**:

	Object
Fred dreamed	that he was travelling to the moon.
I know	that two and two make four.
Mary said	that she liked reading books.

These **clauses** are **objects** of **verbs**. Test them if you like. You remember the test for objects, don't you? You put the question word *what?* after the verb.

verb → what? = object

Fred dreamed that he was travelling to the moon.

dreamed → what? = that he was travelling to the moon.
(object)

I know that two and two make four.

know → what? = that two and two make four. (object)

Those clauses, then, are doing the work of a **noun**. They are **noun clauses**.

83

Lesson Twenty

Almost every **noun clause** you meet will be the **object** of a **transitive verb**, usually a verb like *say*, *think*, *believe*, etc. But you will remember that **nouns** are very often the **subject** of a sentence; and sometimes, but not very often, a **noun clause** is the **subject** of a sentence.

Here are two **simple sentences** each with a **noun** for the **subject**:

Subject	
Your work	seems very difficult.
The prisoner's escape	is a complete mystery.

Now, instead of the noun *work* and the noun *escape* we will use a **clause** that is doing exactly the same work, acting as **subject** of the verb *seems* and the **subject** of the verb *is*:

Subject	
What you are doing	seems very difficult.
How the prisoner escaped	is a complete mystery.

TEACHER: Ann, what work is done by the clauses *What you are doing* and *How the prisoner escaped*?

ANN: The work of a **noun**; each of them is the **subject** of a sentence.

TEACHER: Good. And how do you know they are **dependent clauses**, Grace?

GRACE: Because they have a **verb** in them, so they are not phrases. They don't make complete sense by themselves, so they are not sentences. They form part of a **complex sentence**. They are **noun clauses**.

Noun clauses as the object of a verb

Fred dreamed | that he was travelling to the moon | .

I know | that two and two make four | .

84

Lesson Twenty

Mary said [that she liked reading books].

The **noun clauses** in boxes are the **objects** of the verbs that the arrows point to.

Noun clauses as the subject of a sentence.

[What you are doing] seems very difficult.

[How the prisoner escaped] is a complete mystery.

The **noun clauses** in boxes are the **subjects** of the sentences.

A clause that does the work of a noun in a sentence is a noun clause.

A noun clause is generally the object of a verb or the subject of a sentence.

Exercises

A What does a **noun clause** do?

B Divide these **complex sentences** into **main clauses** and **noun clauses**. Say what work is done by each noun clause. We have done the first one for you. (Number 6 is quite difficult. Write *the teacher replied* in the first column.)

Main clause	Noun clause	Work done by noun clause
1 Fred said	that he was taking Jock for a walk.	object of *said*

1 Fred said that he was taking Jock for a walk.
2 Richard hopes that the teacher won't ask him a question.
3 I believe that you are telling the truth.
4 I have forgotten what your name is.
5 The pupils said that the questions were too difficult.

85

Lesson Twenty

  6 'They are quite easy,' replied the teacher.
  7 Show me how I must do these exercises.
  8 What you said was quite true.
  9 I asked the porter if the train had gone.
10 Why I made that mistake I don't know.

C Complete these sentences by adding a **clause** beginning with *that*.

  1 George said ...
  2 I believe ...
  3 He doesn't think ...
  4 Richard believes ...
  5 Margaret promised ...
  6 I am very much afraid ...
  7 Does John know ...
  8 William heard one day ...
  9 I see ...
10 I certainly hope ...

What kind of clauses have you added?

Lesson Twenty-one

Direct and indirect speech

TEACHER: Where are you, Richard, and what are you doing?
RICHARD: I am in the classroom, and I am writing my exercise.
TEACHER: Joshua, what did Richard say?
JOSHUA: He said that he was in the classroom and was writing his exercise.
TEACHER: What are you holding in your hand, Richard?
RICHARD: I'm holding a pencil.
TEACHER: What did Richard say, Mark?
MARK: He said that he was holding a pencil.
TEACHER: Where are your books, Richard?
RICHARD: They are on my desk.
TEACHER: What did he say, Harry?
HARRY: He said that his books were on his desk.
TEACHER: What time do you come to school, Richard?
RICHARD: I come to school at nine o'clock.
TEACHER: What time did he say he came to school, Lloyd?
LLOYD: He said that he came to school at nine o'clock.
TEACHER: What will you do when you have finished your work, Richard?
RICHARD: I'll go out and play.
TEACHER: What did he say, John?
JOHN: He said that he would go out and play.

In that conversation you had a number of sentences expressed in two ways:
1 By Richard.
2 By the students who reported what Richard said.

Lesson Twenty-one

When you read Richard's words you have the exact words of the speaker. Richard's sentences are **direct speech**.

When you read the words of the other students you have a different form. You don't get the words exactly as Richard said them. You get them as they were reported, indirectly, by another speaker. It is no longer Richard saying 'I', but someone speaking about Richard, and so saying 'he'. And it is not Richard speaking in the **present** time, but someone else, telling you what Richard said in the **past**. The students' sentences are **indirect speech**.

Let us put some of those sentences side by side and see the differences between **direct speech** and **indirect speech**.

Direct	*Indirect*
	The student said that:
I am in the classroom and am writing.	he was in the classroom and was writing.
I'm holding a pencil.	he was holding a pencil.
I come to school at nine o'clock.	he came to school at nine o'clock.
I'll go out and play.	he would go out and play.

Here are some further examples:

Direct	*Indirect*
John said, 'I'm going to London with my father.'	John said that he was going to London with his father.
Margaret said, 'Our train will arrive in five minutes.'	Margaret said that their train would arrive in five minutes.
Gloria said, 'My sister speaks French well.'	Gloria said that her sister spoke French well.
Mary said, 'I hope it won't rain.'	Mary said that she hoped it wouldn't rain.
Lance said, 'I am a student and I have learned grammar for three years.'	Lance said that he was a student and had learned grammar for three years.

Lesson Twenty-one

In every case we can leave out the connecting *that*:

> John said he was going to London with his father.
> Margaret said their train would arrive in five minutes.
> Gloria said her sister spoke French well.
> Mary said she hoped it wouldn't rain.
> Lance said he was a student and had learned grammar for three years.

You will notice that:

1 When a sentence changes from **direct** to **indirect speech**, it is introduced by a verb in the past tense: *He said [that]* ...
2 The **verbs** are changed from **present tense** to **past tense**. The **present perfect** is changed to the **past perfect**.
3 **Pronouns** and **possessive adjectives** in the **1st person** are changed to **pronouns** and **possessive adjectives** in the **3rd person**: *my* and *our* change to *his* or *her* and *their*.
4 In **direct speech** you have quotation marks ('...'). In **indirect speech** you do not.

In general, you have to use common sense in applying the 'rules' for **indirect speech**. For example, Rule 3 isn't right when the person who reports the speech is reporting his or her own speech:

> I said, 'I'll write it down for you.' (direct speech)
> I said I would write it down for them (OR: for you). (indirect speech)

Lesson Twenty-one

And Rule 2 doesn't work when the **direct speech** statement is about something that is always true, or still true:

    Galileo said, 'The earth goes round the sun.' (direct speech)
    Galileo said that the earth goes round the sun. (indirect speech)

    James said, 'I like strawberries.' (direct speech)
    James said he likes strawberries. (indirect speech)

Look at the use of common sense in this case, when the person spoken to is named in the **direct speech**:

    Mary said, 'I've cooked a meal for you, Joyce.' (direct speech)
    Mary said that she had cooked a meal for Joyce. (indirect speech)
    OR: Mary told Joyce that she had cooked a meal for her.

Exercises

A What is the difference between **direct speech** and **indirect speech**? Which has quotation marks, **direct speech** or **indirect speech**?

B When you change sentences from **direct speech** to **indirect speech** what happens to (a) verbs in the **simple present tense**, (b) verbs in the **present perfect tense**, (c) **pronouns** and **possessive adjectives** in the **1st person**?

C Change the following from **direct speech** to **indirect speech**. Begin *He* (*She*, *They*, *Mark*, *Mary*, *The teacher*, etc.) *said* [*that*] . . .

Example: 'I'll give you a lift.'
Answer: She said she would give me a lift.

  1 'I like my dog Jock.'

Lesson Twenty-one

2 'I am going to the party with my brother.'
3 'We have plenty of time to do our work.'
4 'George has written me a long letter.'
5 'We are very tired.'
6 'You sing very nicely, Margaret.'
7 'I am giving a prize for the best homework.'
8 'I am Japanese but I have learned English at school.'
9 'I will take you to my house.'
10 'You can come with us if you like.'
11 'If it rains I'll get wet.'
12 'I am going to give you an exercise on indirect speech. It will not be easy, but if you are thoughtful you can do it, as I have given you all the information you need. You can look in your book if you wish, but I don't want you to ask anyone to help you.'